SPACE EXPLORATION

SCIENCE · TECHNOLOGY · ENGINEERING

BY WIL MARA

CHILDREN'S PRESS®

An Imprint of Scholastic Inc.
New York Toronto London Auckland Sydney
Mexico City New Delhi Hong Kong
Danbury, Connecticut

30

CONTENT CONSULTANT
Kelly Bender, Senior Research Specialist (Mars Space Flight Facility), School of Earth & Space
Exploration, Arizona State University, Tempe

PHOTOGRAPHS ©: Alamy Images: 56 (David Wei), 17 (Design Pics Inc.), 38 (Eddie Gerald),
8 (Everett Collection Inc), 23 (Gary Blake), 42 (Horizons WWP), 4 left, 15 left (Image Asset
Management Ltd.), 10 right (INTERFOTO), 44 (Luc Novovitch), 34 (Marvin Dembinsky Photo
Associates), 55 (Photri Images), 5 right, 50, 52 left, 57 (RGB Ventures/Superstock), 35
(Stephen Frink Collection), 16, 18 (Stocktrek Images, Inc.), 10 left (Trinity Mirror/Mirrorpix);
AP Images: 52 right (Mikhail Metzel), 37 (Reed Saxon); Corbis Images/Gene Blevins: 49
right; ESA/NASA: 24 top, 25 top; Getty Images: 5 left, 43 (Denver Post), 24 bottom (Hyoung
Chang); iStockphoto: 9 (EduardHarkonen), 22 (Viktar); Media Bakery: 54 (Stocktrek Images),
26; NASA: 58 right, 59 left (JPL-Caltech), cover, 4 right, 11, 13, 15 right, 19, 20, 25
bottom, 27, 28, 29 left, 30, 40; Science Source: 47 (Allen Green), 53 (Paul Wootton), 12
(RIA Novosti), 48 left (Scaled Composites), 39 (Spencer Sutton), 3, 6, 31, 32, 36 left, 46,
51; Shutterstock, Inc.: 58 left (David Acosta Allely), 36 right (OtnaYdur); Superstock, Inc.: 59
right (Mark Williamson/Science Faction), 29 right, 48 right, 49 left (NASA/Science Faction);
The Image Works/Lightroom/NASA/TopFoto: 14.

LIBRARY OF CONGRESS CATALOGING-IN-PUBLICATION DATA
Mara, Wil, author.
  Space exploration : science, technology, and engineering / by Wil Mara.
    pages cm. — (Calling all innovators : a career for you?)
  Audience: 9–12.
  Includes bibliographical references and index.
  ISBN 978-0-531-20615-7 (lib. bdg.) — ISBN 978-0-531-21074-1 (pbk.)
  1. Space flight — Juvenile literature. 2. Space flight — History — Juvenile literature. 3.
Astronautics — Juvenile literature. 4. Outer space — Exploration — Juvenile literature. 5. Outer
space — Exploration — History — Juvenile literature. I. Title.
  TL793.M29 2014
  629.4 — dc23   2014003569

All rights reserved. Published in 2015 by Children's Press, an imprint of Scholastic Inc.
Printed in the United States of America 113

1 2 3 4 5 6 7 8 9 10 R 24 23 22 21 20 19 18 17 16 15

S cience, technology, engineering, arts, and math are the fields that drive innovation. Whether they are finding ways to make our lives easier or developing the latest entertainment, the people who work in these fields are changing the world for the better. Do you have what it takes to join the ranks of today's greatest innovators? Read on to discover whether space exploration is a career for you.

TABLE *of* CONTENTS

Astronaut Neil Armstrong was the first person to walk on the moon.

The first seven NASA astronauts were: front row, left to right, Walter M. "Wally" Schirra Jr., Donald K. "Deke" Slayton, John H. Glenn Jr., and M. Scott Carpenter; back row, Alan B. Shepard Jr., Virgil I. "Gus" Grissom, and L. Gordon Cooper Jr.

Aerospace engineer Joe Krampert prepares to move a spacecraft to a testing facility.

NASA's Dawn *spacecraft launches in 2007.*

Astronaut Robert Stewart moves through outer space near the space shuttle Challenger, *with the help of a propulsion backpack.*

CHAPTER ONE

BLASTING OFF

Throughout history, humans have looked to the stars and pondered the question, "What's out there?" The heavenly bodies that we gaze upon every night have long inspired wonder, awe, and imagination.

For centuries, humans could only study the objects in the sky that they could see from the surface of Earth. Then, in the mid-20th century, people were finally able to reach outside Earth's atmosphere. Ever since then, we have studied far off stars and planets, photographed alien landscapes, glimpsed at other galaxies, and pushed humans to the limits of survival.

And this is only the beginning. In less than 100 years, the desire to search, explore, and understand outer space has produced some of the most inspiring moments of the modern age. It has driven us to reach down and find our courage as we strive to achieve our most epic feats. Such is mankind's incredible fascination with worlds that lay beyond our own.

MAJOR MILESTONES

1942	1961	1969	1995
A V2 rocket becomes the first man-made craft to travel into outer space.	Soviet cosmonaut Yuri Gagarin becomes the first human to travel into outer space.	U.S. astronaut Neil Armstrong becomes the first human to walk on the moon.	Russian astronaut Valeri Polyakov sets a record for the longest time spent in space: 437 days.

IN THE BEGINNING

Many historians pinpoint the beginning of human space exploration as October 3, 1942. That was when a V2 rocket became the first man-made object to successfully enter outer space. In October 1946, American scientists used V2s to take the first images of Earth from outer space. The following year, fruit flies became the first living creatures intentionally launched into space by humans. The fruit flies survived the trip and returned to Earth in a capsule with the aid of a parachute.

WERNHER VON BRAUN

The V2 rocket was designed by German scientist Wernher von Braun during World War II (1939–1945). After the war ended, von Braun left Germany for the United States, where he helped develop the U.S. space program.

Wernher von Braun worked with the U.S. space program until the 1970s.

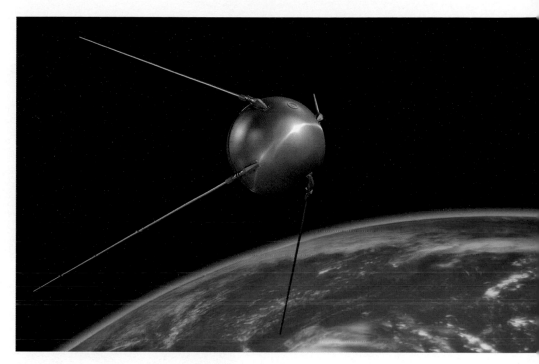

Sputnik 1 *orbited Earth for 92 days before burning up in the planet's atmosphere.*

THE SPACE RACE

The 1950s were a crucial time in the history of space exploration. In the years following World War II, tensions grew between the United States and the Soviet Union. At the same time, the idea of traveling into space was seeming more like a reality every day. The Americans and the Soviets began desperately trying to outdo each other in the "space race" to prove which society was truly superior.

In October 1957, Soviet scientists scored an important victory in the space race by launching the first man-made **satellite**, *Sputnik 1*, into **orbit**. *Sputnik 1* collected a variety of data and sent radio signals back to Earth. The project's success established the Soviet Union as a scientific superpower. In January 1958, the United States struck back with a satellite of its own, called *Explorer 1*. It was more technologically advanced and was able to collect more detailed data than *Sputnik 1*.

THE V2

Wernher von Braun did not have space travel in mind when he designed the V2 rocket. The rocket's original purpose was to be a weapon. It was the first long-range missile, and its intended first target was London, England. German forces launched more than 3,000 V2s throughout the second half of World War II. It is believed that the missiles killed thousands of people during the war, both soldiers and civilians. In addition, thousands of prisoners died after they were forced to assemble the missiles, because the materials used were highly dangerous.

The V2 rocket was a groundbreaking weapon.

Gas masks supplied safe air, protecting a person from dangerous poison gases during the war.

INSPIRATIONAL MASKS

The V2 wasn't the only wartime innovation that contributed to space exploration. The gas masks used in World War II became an inspiration for oxygen delivery systems used in early space suits. The fear of chemical and biological weapon attacks was particularly intense during World War II because such weapons had been widely used during World War I (1914–1918). As a result, defense developers believed there was a need to update and improve gas mask technology. World War II masks were much more comfortable, offered a greater viewing area, and had filters that were more efficient and could be changed more easily. This technology was useful when it came time to design space suits in the following years.

ALWAYS WEAR A HELMET

You have probably seen images of astronauts wearing those big, round helmets, right? Those helmets have been around, in one form or another, since the 1820s. The earliest ones were created to protect firemen when they entered smoke-filled buildings. That version of the helmet was made of copper and had a long leather hose. On the other end of the hose, someone used a hand-operated device called a bellows to pump oxygen into the helmet. By the end of the 1820s, the helmet's inventors realized their helmet might also be useful for diving deep underwater. When space exploration became a reality more than 100 years later, space suit designers took inspiration from these early helmets and their air hoses. ✳

A gold-coated visor protects an astronaut's eyes from the heat and light of the sun when he or she spends time outside a spacecraft.

Yuri Gagarin's 1961 spaceflight was his only trip into space.

HUMANS IN SPACE

The Soviet Union scored another point in the space race in the early 1960s when it sent the first human into outer space. The stunning achievement motivated the United States to speed up its own efforts. The following year, the United States launched the first interplanetary **probe**, *Mariner 2*. The probe flew past the planet Venus that December. It collected a great deal of new information about Venus and about space travel in general.

YURI GAGARIN

On April 12, 1961, Yuri Alekseyevich Gagarin—an army major, pilot, and cosmonaut (the Soviets' term for an astronaut)—made history when he became the first human to visit outer space. Gagarin completed a full orbit of Earth in a Vostok spacecraft. He remained in space for nearly two hours and returned alive and well.

In 1967, the Soviets reached Venus with a probe of their own. But then came a truly mammoth moment in history. On July 20, 1969, the manned U.S. spacecraft *Apollo 11* landed on the moon. Astronauts Neil Armstrong and Buzz Aldrin explored the moon's surface for nearly 22 hours and returned to Earth safely. It was not just an achievement in space exploration, but also a turning point in the history of humankind.

NEXT STEPS

The first major space event of the 1970s was a sad one. In April 1971, three Soviet cosmonauts suffocated to death when their craft malfunctioned on the return to Earth. Before this tragedy, the cosmonauts had successfully docked their Soyuz spacecraft to the first **space station**, *Salyut*, launched earlier that year. Their mission was to experience and gather data about living conditions on the station.

In May 1973, the United States launched its own space station, *Skylab*. It remained in orbit for more than six years. During this time, nine different astronauts carried out hundreds of experiments and lived on the station for a total of 171 days.

In the summer of 1976, two U.S. crafts named *Viking 1* and *Viking 2* became the first man-made objects to reach the surface of Mars. The crafts took photographs, collected soil samples, and gathered other important information about the Red Planet. In August 1979, the U.S. *Pioneer 11* probe reached the orbit of the planet Saturn with the purpose of studying Saturn's **atmosphere** from space.

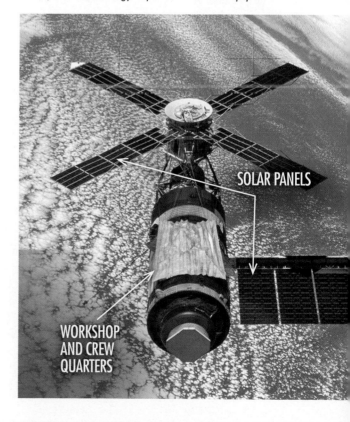

Skylab, *the first space station launched by the United States, used solar energy to power some of its equipment.*

SOLAR PANELS

WORKSHOP AND CREW QUARTERS

THE BIRTH OF AN AGENCY

In 1958, the United States established what would soon become one of the most significant organizations in the history of space exploration—the National Aeronautics and Space Administration. Better known as NASA, the program was born on July 29, 1958, when President Dwight D. Eisenhower signed the National Aeronautics and Space Act into law. Eisenhower's signature turned one of the most ambitious ideas in human history into reality. Since then, NASA has been responsible for many of the greatest achievements in the history of space exploration.

President Dwight Eisenhower (center) meets with NASA's first administrator, Keith Glennan (right), and deputy administrator, Hugh Dryden (left).

Astronaut Neil Armstrong and Edwin "Buzz" Aldrin placed an American flag at their landing site on the moon.

ONE SMALL STEP

Perhaps NASA's greatest accomplishment (so far!) was the first step ever taken by a human being on the surface of the moon. This occurred on July 21, 1969, when astronaut Neil Armstrong stepped off the ladder from *Apollo 11* and into the pages of history. Video footage of the extraordinary event was relayed to Earth live, where millions watched it on television. Although many other astronauts have traveled to the moon since then, the first moonwalk is still considered one of greatest accomplishments of the 20th century.

GOING INTERNATIONAL

The space race between the United States and the Soviet Union eventually ended. It was replaced by a new age of cooperation among the space exploration agencies of many nations. Perhaps the greatest example of this has been the *International Space Station*. This space station is the largest man-made object in space and was launched in 1998. The first craft to formally dock with it was *Expedition 1* in late 2000. Since then, it has been in continual operation and is shared by five space agencies—NASA, the Russian Federal Space Agency, the Japan Aerospace Exploration Agency, the Canadian Space Agency, and the European Space Agency (ESA). ☀

The crew members of Expedition 1 *pose together in 2000.*

REACHING FARTHER

In April 1981, the United States broke new ground again with the launch of an entirely new type of spacecraft—the space shuttle. One of the main features of the shuttle was its airplane-like design. This was created in part so the shuttle could land like an airplane upon its return. This made it reusable, unlike previous spacecraft.

In 1977, the United States' probes *Voyager 1* and *Voyager 2* were launched. Throughout the 1980s, the two began sending back groundbreaking data from their missions to explore the outermost planets in our **solar system**. *Voyager 2* reached Jupiter in July 1979, then Saturn in August 1981. It also reached Uranus in January 1986 and Neptune in August 1989. In 1986, probes from different nations were sent to study Halley's Comet, which only passes by Earth about once every 75 years. The United States, the Soviet Union, Japan, and the ESA all sent probes.

Voyager 2 flew by Neptune in August 1989, as shown in this illustration.

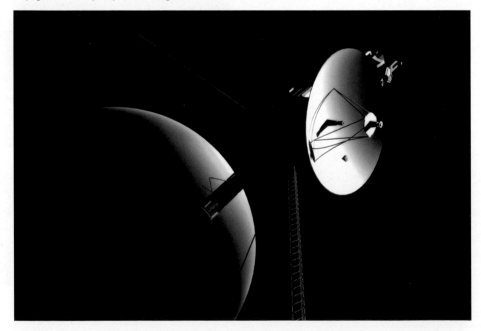

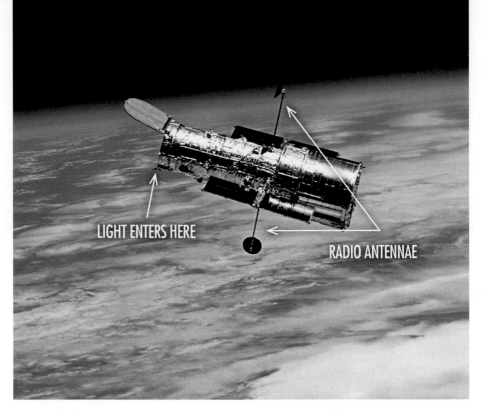

LIGHT ENTERS HERE

RADIO ANTENNAE

The design, construction, and launch of the Hubble Telescope was one of NASA's most ambitious missions.

LEARNING ABOUT SPACE ITSELF

In 1990, NASA launched the Hubble Telescope into Earth's orbit. It featured a variety of state-of-the-art cameras and other cutting-edge instruments that allowed scientists to observe faraway parts of space that had never been studied before.

In August of the same year, the *Magellan* probe began using **radar** signals to map the surface of Venus. In 1992, two **astronomers**, Aleksander Wolszczan and Dale Frail, discovered proof that planets exist beyond our solar system. NASA recorded another success in 1997 when the *Pathfinder* craft landed on the surface of Mars. Among other remarkable discoveries was evidence suggesting that Mars might have once been home to water. This raised the possibility that the planet could support life. *Pathfinder* also sent back images of the Martian surface that were astonishingly detailed.

Spirit *is one of the rovers studying the Martian landscape.*

INTO THE NEW MILLENNIUM

In 2003, NASA launched two **rover** vehicles to further explore the surface of Mars. Both reached the Martian surface in January 2004. One of the goals was to confirm the possibility that water had previously existed on Mars. The findings of the two vehicles—named *Spirit* and *Opportunity*—seemed to point strongly to this conclusion.

In 2004, the NASA craft *Cassini* safely reached the orbit of Saturn, years after its 1997 launch. Attached to the craft was a probe called *Huygens*. *Huygens* detached from *Cassini* and landed on the surface of Titan, a moon of Saturn. It then began sending back images of Titan's surface and information about its atmosphere. It also provided evidence supporting the belief that there could be some kind of liquid on Titan's surface.

In May 2008, NASA successfully landed yet another craft on Mars. Named *Phoenix*, this craft was tasked with exploring the colder regions of the planet. It returned final proof that water, in the form of ice, existed just below the Martian surface. And in March 2009, NASA began the ambitious Kepler Mission by launching a telescope capable of locating Earthlike planets well beyond our solar system. More than 700 such potential planets were found within the first few years of the project.

WE ARE (PROBABLY) NOT ALONE

The year 2010 was thrilling for space enthusiasts. In late September, a group of American astronomers announced that they had discovered the first planet that seemed able to support life-forms, as we know them, on its surface. The planet, which researchers named Gliese 581g (nicknamed Zarmina), is located far beyond our solar system. Scientists believe it to be roughly 33 percent larger than Earth. It does not seem to rotate on an **axis**, however. This means one side of Zarmina is always facing its sun and the other side is always dark. This means the side facing its sun is very hot, and the dark side facing away is very cold. However, temperatures along the line between day and night, called the **terminator**, might be mild enough for life to exist.

In August 2011, NASA once again turned the public's attention to Mars when it made the announcement that it had found flowing water on the planet's surface. This makes it very possible that life once existed on the planet and could perhaps exist there even now. Around a year later, NASA successfully landed a rover called *Curiosity* on Mars. Scientists are hoping it will open the door to the possibility of human travel to Mars in the not-too-distant future.

People around the world were excited about the news that Mars has liquid water.

The space shuttle, used between 1981 and 2011, was the world's first reusable spacecraft.

2

TODAY AND TOMORROW

While humans have long dreamed of traveling to faraway worlds, it has only been in relatively recent times that we have succeeded in doing so. After those first stages of space exploration, we are now searching for new goals as we look even farther and set our ambitions ever higher. Researchers peer more closely at the places we have been and search deeper into space, past the Moon, our solar system, into the Milky Way, and beyond. Just as we have conquered so many seemingly impossible challenges here on our home planet, we hope to one day conquer the frontiers of space that once seemed unreachable. It won't be easy, but space explorers will continue the process one small step at a time.

PROPOSED FUTURE SPACE MISSIONS

2020	2035	2045	2100
The first permanent base could be established on the moon.	Humans could set foot on Mars for the first time.	A base could be established on Jupiter's moon Callisto.	Probes that can reach and contact other planetary systems could be launched.

THE MAPMAKERS

In 2013, the ESA took steps toward the goal of creating a complete map of the Milky Way **galaxy**. The mission, called Gaia, kicked off with the successful launch of a two-telescope probe on December 19. The probe reached a point just beyond Earth's orbit around the sun and began collecting data. It has equipment designed to protect it from the sun's intensity while also converting the sun's rays into energy. Its two telescopes scan the entire galaxy by rotating once every six hours. Astronomers are hoping the data collected by the probe will reveal the secrets of the Milky Way's origins. The mission is scheduled to conclude in 2021.

A portion of the Milky Way appears as a thick band of stars in the sky on Earth.

Virgin Galactic first revealed its tourist spaceship design in 2009.

ALL ABOARD!

Ever dreamed of traveling through space? Well, that dream could turn into reality in the 21st century. Space tourism looks to become a very big thing in the coming years. One of the companies leading the way is Virgin Galactic. It was founded in 2004 as part of the larger Virgin Group, a collection of businesses owned by British billionaire Richard Branson. A longtime fan of space travel, Branson began Virgin Galactic with the purpose of providing non-astronauts the opportunity to visit outer space.

Virgin Galactic's space tourism program is still being developed. Its spacecraft have been built and are continuing test flights before they can be deemed safe enough for passengers. When that time comes, tourist flights will be suborbital. This means they will go into space and fly a certain distance but will not make a complete orbit around Earth. Branson and other space tourism pioneers hope that one day they will be able to take their passengers well beyond Earth's atmosphere. Possible destinations could include the moon or Mars. For the time being, however, a quick jaunt around our blue planet will have to do.

FROM THIS TO THAT

UP, UP, AND AWAY!

With the rapid development of the space tourism industry, there needs to be a place where "spaceplanes" can land and take off. The first place that this appears to be happening is on the grounds of Colorado's Front Range Airport, which lies east of Denver. The airport's administrators have taken steps to make this airport the site of the world's first spaceport. If all goes according to plan, flights to and from space will work much like typical airplane flights at any other airport. Ongoing studies are being conducted to see how this can all work out smoothly, and the first flights are planned to take place in 2014 or 2015. Get your tickets now!

A NEW WAY TO TRAVEL

In 2011, NASA and the ESA announced their development of a manned spacecraft called the *Orion Multipurpose Crew Vehicle* (*MPCV*). The *MPCV* will utilize the latest technology to send manned missions to the moon, various **asteroids**, and the *International Space Station*. It will also be able to complete unmanned missions, including the transport of supplies to the space station.

The *MPCV* can accommodate no more than six astronauts at a time, and manned flights are not expected to begin until 2020. However, if successful, the craft will likely lead to the first manned mission to Mars.

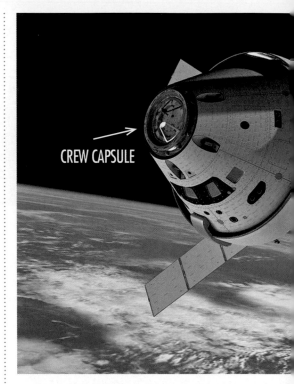

CREW CAPSULE

Before it carries people, Orion will be tested with an unmanned spaceflight, planned for 2017.

The Front Range Airport in Colorado could make history as the first spaceport.

SERVICE MODULE
SUPPLIES POWER,
WATER, AND OTHER
NECESSITIES

NOT QUITE PLANETS

In 2015, NASA will once again be responsible for a space-exploration first. The probe known as *Dawn*, launched in September 2007, will reach the **dwarf planet** Ceres. Ceres was first noted in 1801. At the time, it was thought to be a full-sized planet. It is of particular interest to astronomers because it has an icy surface and may possess an underground ocean. This means there is a possibility that it could support some form of life. It currently follows an orbit that takes it between Mars and Jupiter. It completes one orbit roughly every four and a half Earth years ☀

Researchers hope to gain information about the evolution of planets with the help of Dawn.

PARACHUTE TO SLOW
CURIOSITY'S DESCENT

The Mars rover Curiosity *landed in the Gale Crater in 2012.*

WATER, WATER EVERYWHERE

Scientists continue to find evidence of water on the surface of Mars.
In late 2013, it was announced that a huge crater on the Martian
surface is most likely the site of a former lake. Further, there are
mountains on Mars that appear to have water currently on their
slopes. This suggests strongly that there was a time when Mars was
able to support life. Scientists are continuing to look for evidence to
support this theory. They are searching mainly for certain **organic**
materials, especially those that contain carbon. So far, they have
found samples of both carbon dioxide and nitric oxide. These
substances contain carbon and nitrogen, which are two things that
life-forms need to survive.

NOT JUST MARS

Mars isn't the only place in our solar system that is believed to contain bodies of water. One of Jupiter's moons, Europa, may have an ocean under its frozen surface. In late 2013, scientists spotted what they believe to be **geysers** of water shooting up from Europa's extreme southern region. Some are even theorizing that an underground ocean could be helping to support alien life-forms. The geysers were spotted with the aid of the famous Hubble Telescope. They were believed to reach as high as 125 miles (201 kilometers) above the surface. Scientists are continuing to watch Europa in hopes of seeing more geysers in the future. The ESA plans to send a probe to explore Jupiter, Europa, and Jupiter's other moons sometime in 2022. In addition, Europa is not the only moon believed by experts to have an underground ocean. Many believe Saturn's moon Enceladus also has a massive ocean that separates its icy surface from its **core**.

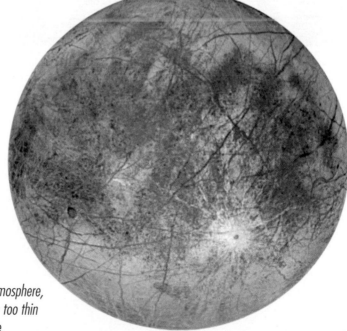

Europa has oxygen in its atmosphere, but the atmosphere is much too thin to allow a person to breathe.

MODERN MARVELS

Space suits have come a long way since those worn by the first U.S. astronauts in the early 1960s.

SUITING UP

Space suits have gone through significant improvements since their earliest days. The first space suits were based on equipment used by divers, soldiers, and airplane pilots. As a result, early space suits had some problems dealing with the demands of space travel. Breathing equipment was sometimes awkward and unreliable. Air tubes became tangled around other items or even broke during missions. In addition, most helmets were fixed in place. This made it difficult for astronauts to see around themselves. Gloves were thick, making it difficult for astronauts to rely on their sense of touch. Today's space suits have been much improved since the days of this outdated technology. They are equipped with lightweight breathing gear and have tremendous flexibility, improved protection from environmental extremes, and advanced communication capabilities.

Pieces, or modules, could be added to or removed from Mir.

THE FLOATING WORLD

Space stations have also seen incredible advances since the earliest ones were launched. The first true space station was the Soviet *Salyut 1*, launched in 1971. It was intended to be used for a brief period and then abandoned. In later years, improved versions of the *Salyut* design included docking facilities. This enabled crews to come and go more freely. The early U.S. space station *Skylab* also had docking capabilities. The first truly modern station was the Soviet *Mir*, which launched in 1986. Its **modular** design allowed it to be made smaller or larger as needed. Today's space stations still use modular designs and are not abandoned like early space stations were.

PROBING OUR WAY AROUND

Humankind has been sending probes into space for some time now. A probe is an unmanned spacecraft sent to collect data and relay it back to Earth. This data can take many forms, including photographs, rock or soil samples, weather readings, and more. The greatest value of a probe is that no human lives are at stake. The first probe sent successfully into space was the Soviet *Sputnik 1*, launched in 1957. It was a fairly simple device—a smallish metal ball, less than 2 feet (61 centimeters) in diameter, with four antennae to send back radio signals. Since *Sputnik 1*, many other probes have been launched by the world's various space agencies. Today's probe technology is quite different. Modern probes have advanced communication and mobility systems. They also contain a wide array of data-collecting equipment, making them able to provide far more detailed information than earlier probes. ✳

A 2009 mission crashed two probes into Earth's moon in search of water.

LOOKING INTO THE PAST

In July 2008, NASA began construction on the powerful new Webb telescope, with help from both the ESA and the Canadian Space Agency. The Webb telescope is expected to replace the Hubble in 2014. While the Hubble has played an important role in space exploration, the Webb telescope is far superior technologically. Its main purpose will be an attempt to observe and gather data about the very origins of the universe. It will provide information about how stars, planets, galaxies, and other heavenly bodies are formed. Scientists are also hoping it will identify new planets capable of supporting life-forms similar to our own. The Webb is planned for a five-year mission, but it could possibly remain in space for as long as 10 years if it remains operational. It will most likely be sent into orbit around the sun. The telescope is named for James Webb, who ran NASA from 1961 to 1968.

The Webb telescope looks very different from Hubble.

PRIMARY OPTICAL TELESCOPE MIRROR

SECONDARY MIRROR

SUNSHIELD

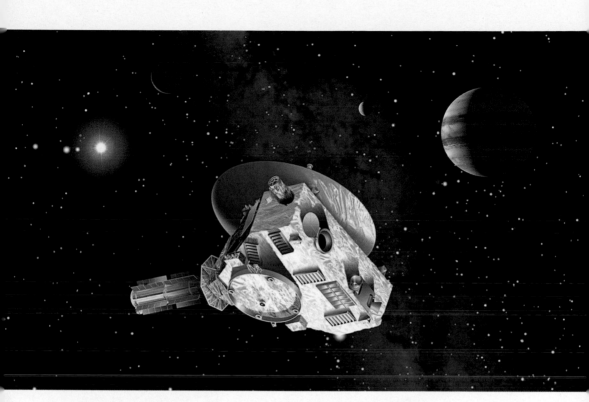

New Horizons *must travel more than 3 billion miles (4.8 billion km) to reach Pluto.*

THE ENDS OF THE SOLAR SYSTEM

In January 2006, NASA launched a speedy little craft known as *New Horizons*. Since that time, *New Horizons* has been doing just one thing—hurtling through space toward the dwarf planet Pluto. Pluto is one of the last major bodies in our solar system that has not been studied closely. When the craft reaches its destination in July 2015, it will study both Pluto and its only moon, Charon. Once it has completed its study of Pluto and Charon, *New Horizons* will continue onward to explore the Kuiper Belt, which lies at the most distant edge of the solar system. In many ways, this part of its mission is even more historic than its examination of Pluto and Charon. Little is known about the Kuiper Belt beyond the fact that it is populated by a variety of dark, frozen objects.

A technician inspects Mars Science Laboratory, and the rover Curiosity packed inside it, in preparation for its launch.

ON THE JOB

For some people, fascination with space exploration will never be anything more than a hobby to keep up with from the comfort of home. From Web sites, to television programs, to backyard telescopes, these enthusiasts have a lot of resources to help them keep an eye on recent discoveries and ongoing research. Others, however, want to be in the thick of things. For them, the need to know more about what lies beyond Earth's atmosphere will launch a career in space exploration. Such a career is not made easily. If you are thinking of devoting your life to studying the far reaches of outer space, you will need a love of science and mathematics. You will also need a willingness to work very hard. Space agencies only hire the best and the brightest. Human lives as well as billions of dollars are usually at stake on space missions. However, for many people, the possible discoveries to be made in space exploration are well worth the time and effort!

SPACE EXPLORATION DISASTERS

1967	1967	1986	2003
A fire during a test of the Apollo 1 spacecraft results in the death of three astronauts.	Cosmonaut Vladimir Mikhaylovich Komarov is killed when the parachute on his return craft fails to open.	Seven American astronauts are killed when space shuttle Challenger explodes less than three minutes after takeoff because of a fuel leak.	Seven American astronauts die when space shuttle Columbia breaks apart during reentry.

Time spent outside a spacecraft is called Extravehicular Activity, or EVA.

I WANT TO BE AN ASTRONAUT!

Who wouldn't want to zip through space in a rocket ship, traveling beyond Earth's atmosphere and flying around the moon? This is what an astronaut does. But as fun and exciting as this sounds, make no mistake—it is not easy to become a NASA astronaut. To begin with, you need a graduate degree in a field such as science, engineering, or mathematics. Commander and pilot astronauts also need at least 1,000 hours of flight experience as jet pilots.

In addition to this advanced training and education, NASA astronauts must meet several other requirements. They must be U.S. citizens. They must also have perfect vision, be in excellent health, and meet height requirements.

TIME FOR TRAINING

Even after meeting the strict requirements for becoming an astronaut, there is still a long way to go before potential astronauts are allowed to travel into space. The NASA training program lasts for nearly two years. During this time, trainees get used to the experience of space travel using flight simulations as well as actual flights in high-speed aircraft. They also spend time in zero gravity chambers so they can get used to feeling weightless. They must study and take tests to prove they understand the ins and outs of space travel.

Once a new astronaut has passed through this intense training program, there is still no guarantee that he or she will be blasting off anytime soon. Since the beginning of space travel, just over 500 people have ever made their way into outer space. But for the true space fanatic, becoming an astronaut is the stuff of dreams.

Astronauts train underwater to prepare for the low gravity they would experience during a visit to an asteroid.

Artwork shows what a proposed spacecraft might look like.

VISIONS OF THE FUTURE

When planning new missions, NASA administrators must propose their ideas to the government to ask for the funds they need. Images can be very helpful in persuading government officials that a mission is worthwhile. This is where concept artists come in. These remarkably talented people gather as much information as they can about the proposal, then create illustrations designed to stir the soul and amaze the mind. Some artists use computer software to create their images, while others use more traditional art forms, such as painting or drawing. It's one thing to be told about a probe that will visit Venus or Jupiter. It's another thing altogether to see a vibrant, full-color picture of the craft in action.

Artists might draw an illustration digitally using a tablet.

PUBLIC RELATIONS

Public relations (PR) experts occupy some of the most creative positions in a space agency. PR workers are responsible for informing people about a space agency's business. They are also in charge of getting the public interested and excited about space missions. There are many ways to do this. A smart PR person knows, for example, which photographs of the latest mission to Mars to release to the news media and how to make a future mission sound like the most incredible event in human history. PR pros create exciting presentations for schools and other institutions, maintain Web sites, and deal with reporters and other members of the media. They are a space agency's message makers—and spreading just the right message requires quite a bit of creativity. ✴

NASA holds press conferences, where employees explain to the public how a mission will work and what researchers hope to learn.

STARING INTO THE STARS

Astronauts aren't the only people who spend their careers studying outer space. Many of the most important space discoveries in history were made by astronomers right here on Earth. An astronomer collects and analyzes data about everything from planets and moons to stars and asteroids. Professional astronomers need advanced education in subjects such as physics, mathematics, and chemistry. It is rare today to find a professional astronomer who has not earned a doctorate degree.

While astronomers may not travel into space, they often travel to research posts around the world. Astronomers are not limited to working for governmental space agencies either. They can also find jobs at private research organizations or universities. Some will be called upon to manage observatories and help design research equipment. Their main goal is still the same, however—a quest for answers in a universe loaded with mysteries.

An astronomer watches images from the Wise Observatory in the Negev Desert in Israel.

Some astrophysicists study the mechanics of black holes.

SPACE SPECIALTIES

Astrophysics is a branch of astronomy that focuses on the physical properties of objects in space. An astrophysicist studies planets, moons, and other celestial bodies to find out what they are made of, where they came from, and how they relate to other nearby objects. An astrophysicist may be asked to propose a theory on the possibilities of time travel, the dangers that a black hole poses to Earth, or the origins of the universe. These things might sound like something out of a *Star Trek* movie, but they are very real indeed.

Astrobiologists study the possibility of life on other planets. They search for worlds that might be home to alien life-forms as well as places where humans might one day be able to live. With unmanned spacecraft now traveling to the very ends of our solar system, plus telescopes capable of observing planets well outside of our galaxy, astrobiology is becoming more and more important.

Jill Prince is the NASA Engineering and Safety Center chief engineer at the NASA Langley Research Center.

When did you start thinking about getting into the field of space exploration? What was it about this discipline that interested/ inspired you? When I was in fifth grade, I was involved in a summer program where students would take a variety of classes. . . . One of my classes was astronomy, and the teacher went out of his way to get the kids involved and inspired. One evening he invited the entire class to his house, where he had built an observatory. . . . I distinctly remember seeing the rings of Saturn through one of his telescopes, and I was immediately hooked.

What kinds of classes did you take in middle school, high school, and beyond to prepare for your career? I did not spend my childhood or adolescence preparing for a career. I took classes that I thought were interesting and/ or fun. I did well in math, so I chose to take advanced math classes, but I also, however, liked to stretch the other part of my brain. . . . I went to college undecided in my major, but I leaned towards psychology and maybe even music. My freshman adviser in college was an astronomer, though, and in discussions with him, I eventually fell back onto my early interests in astronomy. . . . I ended up majoring in physics with a concentration in astronomy. Even upon earning a degree in physics, I was still undecided where my career would take me, until a mere suggestion from a researcher was made to consider engineering.

What other projects and jobs did you do in school and your work life before beginning your career? And how did that work prepare you? In college, in addition to classwork, I volunteered time in an astrophysics lab.

. . . [Once,] I was asked to be part of [a telescope part] installation . . . at the South Pole! It was my first Christmas away from family, but it was one of the most exciting times of my life.

My graduate classes were largely taught by George Washington University faculty, my research was with NASA. Upon graduation, I was immediately asked to support a flight project during mission operations . . . This immediate on-the-job training was absolutely essential in springboarding my career.

Do you have a particular project that you're especially proud of or that you think really took your work to another level? I am particularly proud of the work I did with the Mars *Phoenix* lander entry, descent, and landing (EDL) phase. . . . I had to juggle quite a bit in the five years I supported this mission. During the first couple of years of my Phoenix support (2003–2006), I was already working on another flight project, the Mars Reconnaissance Orbiter. Toward the end (2007–2008), I also took on another role as the assistant branch head of the group I was working in. . . . I take pride in maintaining my sanity with all of this going on. The other major reason I'm proud of this work is that it was a really great team effort.

It obviously takes teamwork to make things happen in the field of space exploration. Does working as part of a team come naturally to you, or was it something you had to learn and work on? A little of both. . . . What I have had to learn and work on is that [an] answer I came up with might not be the only or best answer. Or maybe it is the "right" answer, but there may be several "right" ways of getting there. The art of compromise is a valuable and essential tool in any industry, and it requires constant attention for one to grow as an engineer and a leader.

What would your dream project be if you were given unlimited resources? There is so much we could do with unlimited resources! At the top of my personal list would be landing humans on the surface of Mars and returning them safely to Earth. I think we'll get there in my lifetime, but with a higher budget we could speed up the technology development we need to make it work.

What advice would you give to a young person who wants to do what you do one day? Keep an open mind! There are a lot of different possibilities out there. I did not know at age 10 that I wanted to be a NASA engineer. I took opportunities when they presented themselves, and when they didn't I found them. . . . Keeping an open mind and occasionally taking a different path than the obvious makes the journey more interesting.

Engineers at the European Space Agency discuss the results of a test on a new spacecraft.

OUTER SPACE ENGINEERS

Designing and building spacecraft is where creativity comes into play in the space exploration business. The people who design these technological marvels are known as aerospace engineers. They study existing craft in hopes of continually making improvements with the next generation. They pore over design documents and spend hundreds of hours testing new ideas. They are responsible for understanding every factor that will affect a craft's abilities, from **propulsion** systems to the devices used to collect information about climate and geology. This means their education needs to be varied and extensive. An aerospace engineer might study everything from physics and mathematics to computers and chemistry. In addition to education, all engineers need creativity and an ability to think outside the box.

KEEPING EVERYTHING IN ORDER

Once a spacecraft is built, it must be kept in working order. The people responsible for maintaining and repairing spacecraft are called aerospace technicians. These technicians have to make certain that a spacecraft's moving parts are in working order, that its computer systems don't have glitches, and much more. They conduct extensive tests on every craft before and after each mission. They then decide which parts need to be adjusted, updated, or replaced. An aerospace technician's checklist can contain hundreds, if not thousands, of things that need to be done for each mission. Each one of these tasks is just as important as the next. The safety of astronauts aboard a manned craft depends on aerospace technicians doing their job correctly. Aerospace technicians also take part in the creation of new spacecraft, from the planning and design to the testing stage.

An aerospace technician prepares the Orion MPCV and its launch system for a performance test.

Spacecraft are built in clean rooms, which are kept as dust-free as possible. Workers wear special coveralls to help keep the room clean.

4

IF YOU BUILD IT, THEY WILL FLY

From the earliest days of space exploration, engineers, scientists, and other experts have consistently worked to improve the technology used to study the stars. Even with all of our past successes, there is still a lot left to learn about space travel.

It is an ongoing process of discovery through trial and error. There will always be a need to make equipment that is faster, more lightweight, and more durable. Engineers are also constantly looking for ways to make spacecraft perform more detailed observations and possibly carry humans over longer and longer distances. The creation of new spacecraft requires enormous amounts of effort, money, and other resources. However, the end results always represent the cutting edge in the field of aerospace engineering.

TREMENDOUS TECHNOLOGY

1957	1971	1981	2012
The first satellite, Sputnik 1, makes a complete orbit around Earth.	The first space station, Salyut 1, is launched.	The first space shuttle, Challenger, is launched.	The U.S. craft Curiosity lands on Mars and is the most advanced space laboratory yet.

If a crew is going to be in space a long time, it needs a place on the spacecraft to eat and store food.

WHAT'S THE PLAN?

The first step of creating a new spacecraft is to decide what its purpose will be. The engineers consider some basic questions about the project. Where is it going? How long will it take to get there? What will it do after it gets there? How long will it be gone? Will it be coming back? Once they answer these and many other questions, they can begin planning what materials it will be made of, how it will be propelled, and what kind of equipment it will carry. For example, if the craft will be performing geologic studies on Mars, it might need equipment for collecting soil samples as well as a way to launch again and return the samples to Earth. A manned spacecraft might need life-support equipment and extra space for the astronauts to move around.

SIMULATING SPACE

Once a craft's purpose and features have been determined, engineers can start designing it. Spacecraft have been built in a startling variety of shapes and sizes. These shapes are not chosen at random or just for looks. Every element of a spacecraft's design has an important purpose. Engineers use math and physics to determine how a spacecraft will move through space. They also examine data collected on past space missions to predict any issues the new craft might encounter on its journey. Computer simulations allow them to test out their ideas long before a spacecraft is actually built.

Engineers spent several years designing the space shuttle, and continued to adjust its design throughout NASA's use of the spacecraft.

WHERE THE MAGIC HAPPENS

THE SPACESHIP COMPANY

The Spaceship Company is a spacecraft manufacturer located in Mojave, California. It was founded in 2005 by billionaire businessperson Richard Branson and veteran aerospace engineer Burt Rutan. The company builds craft both for spaceflight and ordinary air flight. However, its main interest is creating spacecraft that can be used for commercial space tourism. The Spaceship Company's most notable design is called SpaceShipTwo. SpaceShipTwo has an interesting launch process. It is carried into the air by another Spaceship Company creation, the WhiteKnightTwo. It then separates and jets off into space. Eventually, anyone who buys a ticket may be able to travel aboard this incredible craft.

A WhiteKnight aircraft carries SpaceShipTwo on a test flight.

NASA'S IDEA CENTER

The Langley Research Center in Hampton, Virginia, is NASA's oldest research facility. It is where many of NASA's biggest ideas make the jump from fantasy to reality. Langley has been the site of some of the most important events in space exploration history. The first landing on the moon was tested there in simulation exercises. It was

Suspended sideways to simulate the moon's gravity, an astronaut practices for a lunar landing.

also where the first facility for replicating weightlessness was built. Today, Langley engineers and scientists test experimental materials, new methods of propulsion, computer software, and much more. It can be thought of as a playground where the best and brightest minds in the space industry are allowed to let their creativity soar.

FEELING DESERTED

NASA routinely tests its latest and greatest ideas in the deserts of the western United States. These barren areas are the closest in makeup to the surfaces of other planets, that can be found on Earth. NASA can't simply send a rover to Mars and hope for the best. Engineers might load a few different design models into a big truck and bring them out to the dunes of California, Utah, Nevada, Arizona, or New Mexico. There, they can check a vehicle for everything from its ability to gather up samples to how well it responds to remote control commands. Video cameras are perched in numerous spots at a testing site so the results can be studied later on. Obstacles are often placed to give the vehicles the most rigorous challenges possible. ✳

Engineers test out a model of a Mars rover in the Dumont Dunes in California.

PIECE BY PIECE

Once the engineers have settled on a design, they create diagrams and other documents describing the different parts of the craft and how they will be assembled. Almost every part will be created from scratch and customized for a particular vehicle. The raw materials used to build a modern spacecraft are mainly lightweight yet durable metals such as magnesium, titanium, or aluminum. A variety of modern plastics are also utilized.

Engineers carefully consider the relationship between each of the craft's many parts. The average spacecraft is built from hundreds of thousands of bits and pieces. They must all work together for the craft to function correctly. In spite of all the careful planning, it is not unusual for engineers to make adjustments once assembly begins. Everything from the wiring of a computer system to the basic material used on the craft's outer skin can change as the vehicle is built.

Workers take enormous care when constructing spacecraft.

The Orion MPCV is dropped into a basin of water at Langley Research Center to test what happens if it crashes in water.

TEST TIME

Extensive testing begins as the spacecraft nears completion. An amazing variety of tests are performed on each part of the craft long before it goes out the door. Computer systems are subjected to every simulated situation imaginable to be sure they can respond quickly and accurately. Then there are environmental tests. The craft is stressed under extreme temperatures, winds, vibrations, and anything else it might experience on its mission. Then it is transported to a wide-open space where it can go through numerous low-level flights and impact tests. At this stage, propulsion and navigation systems are also examined. Testing is not a quick process. It takes years for a spacecraft to be approved for use on a mission.

It takes a huge amount of energy to lift a rocket off the ground and into space.

GETTING A BOOST

Modern space vehicles are faster, larger, more comfortable, and more efficient than ever before. But some things haven't changed in decades. You've no doubt heard the phrase "blast off." Well, today's spacecraft are still blasting off in more or less the same way that they did half a century ago. Booster rockets are usually attached to space vehicles as "first-stage" liftoff devices. This means they are designed to get the craft off the launchpad, into the sky, and then beyond Earth's atmosphere. After that, the rockets detach and the craft relies on other propulsion systems to reach its destination. Engineers are studying other methods of first-stage propulsion. For now, however, the old way seems to work just fine.

TUNING IN

With all of the incredible technology we have today, many people have forgotten about a little device known as the radio.

Astronauts today, such as Karen Nyberg, still use radio headsets to communicate during certain portions of a mission.

However, radio communication is still used often in space exploration. Radio waves were first transmitted in 1887 by a German physicist named Heinrich Rudolf Hertz. In 1895, Italian inventor Guglielmo Marconi built a unit that could send radio waves over great distances. When the earliest spacecraft were being built, radio waves seemed like the best method of communicating between Earth and outer space. They were usually reliable and very fast, traveling at a speed of more than 186,000 miles per second (300,000 kps). This made radio ideal for communicating with craft that were sitting on the moon or hurtling toward Jupiter or Saturn.

IT'S NOT JUST FOR WRAPPING UP LEFTOVERS

From *Sputnik 1* to the latest and greatest craft sent into space today, the raw material that engineers keep turning to when building spacecraft is aluminum. We see this metal every day in foil wrap, soda cans, bicycles, kitchen utensils, and a whole array of other common items. It is soft and light, yet strong. It also doesn't rust and can withstand very high heat without melting. This makes it ideal for constructing spacecraft and other aircraft. ✷

Layers of material below the Webb Telescope are coated in aluminum. The material protects the telescope from the sun's intensity.

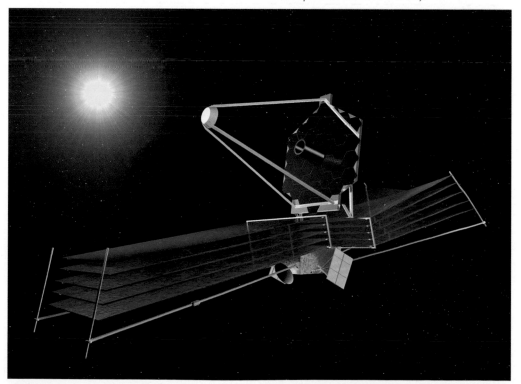

NASA has used the crawler transporter for many different spacecraft, including the space shuttles.

GETTING THERE

Spacecraft builders use a device called a crawler transporter to move huge, heavy spacecraft from the hangar to the launchpad. The crawler transporter is one of the most unusual vehicles in the world. It is a huge platform with rolling, tanklike tracks instead of wheels. There are walkways running all around the platform and several doors leading into small rooms and staircases. It is a lot like a long, flat building that can move from place to place. Spacecraft are set on top of it, then the crawler transporter hauls them to the launch site. A crawler moves very slowly so the spacecraft does not topple over. In fact, the crawler is not able to move any faster than 1 mile per hour (1.6 kph). Only two crawler transporters exist, and they are both located at NASA's Kennedy Space Center. They were built in 1965 and have undergone several upgrades since then.

LETTING GO

The point on Earth where a spacecraft begins its journey into space is called the launchpad. There are generally two main parts to a launchpad—the "umbilical" structures and the "service" structures. The umbilical structures aid technicians in supplying the craft with supplies such as fuel, electricity, and water. Service structures can be moved around the craft. They allow technicians to access different parts of the craft so they can be carefully examined one last time prior to launch. They are also used to load cargo onto the craft. Most launchpad equipment is built to resist great temperatures. This is because first-stage rocket boosters give off unbelievable heat during a launch!

Umbilical and service structures extend from different levels of a tall tower, allowing access to different parts of a spacecraft.

COUNTDOWN

In space movies, there is often a dramatic scene where a steady voice delivers a launch countdown over a loudspeaker: "5 . . . 4 . . . 3 . . . 2 . . . 1 . . . Blast off!" Launching a spacecraft requires more than just a simple countdown, though. The overall countdown process begins when everything and everyone is in place and the final steps before liftoff are being taken. Technicians at the launch center connect with computer systems on the craft, the launch area is cleared of all people and equipment, and final weather readings are taken. Then the first-stage boosters are started. The actual, spoken countdown that we are all familiar with usually only occurs during the final 10 seconds—and the official counter doesn't actually yell "blast off!" as the craft launches.

A control center is a hive of activity before liftoff, as everyone works to complete their assigned tasks.

ONWARD TO THE HEAVENS

When the big moment comes, the spacecraft lifts from its launchpad and begins moving upward. With the noise, the smoke, and the flames shooting out from the rocket, it is a spectacular sight to see. Weather is not the only factor that determines the ideal time for liftoff. It is also determined in large part by Earth's rotation. The mission team chooses a time when the launch site is pointed directly at the craft's destination. This ensures that it can take the most direct route possible.

Once the craft is in the air, it begins to rapidly gain speed. A craft officially reaches outer space as it passes the Kármán Line, which lies 62 miles (100 km) above Earth's surface. From there, it will continue to whatever exciting new destinations await.

Rockets leave a trail of smoke as they blast toward outer space.

BACK TO THE MOON — TO STAY

There are big plans for the space industry in the 21st century, many of which are incredibly ambitious. In 1961, President John F. Kennedy announced that he wanted to send a man to the moon and return him safely to Earth before the end of that decade. Now the moon looks like a desirable goal once again, although for entirely different reasons. NASA has already announced that it would like to establish a permanent base on the moon by 2020. Once the base is completed, it can be used as a kind of pit stop for continuing flights to Mars and perhaps even beyond.

This artist's concept illustration shows the complicated path of the Europa Clipper's orbit.

A CLOSER LOOK

In the coming decades, NASA hopes to make a close and thorough study of Jupiter's moon Europa. Scientists and engineers are at work developing spacecraft to learn about its ocean, icy surface, and atmosphere, and whether the moon could support

As our closest neighbor, the moon is a natural choice for experimenting with the first permanent base outside Earth.

seeing this vision become reality as early as the 2030s. NASA plans to establish a base on Mars where astronauts could live for a year or more at a time. The base would be mobile, enabling the astronauts to move about the planet and study several different regions. At present, it is believed the flight to Mars would take several months. Study targets would include general characteristics of the planet's surface, evidence that life existed there in the past, and, perhaps most exciting of all, the plausibility of further human colonization in the future. ✳

Buildings on Mars will have to offer breathable air and protection from the sun's intensity, which Mars's atmosphere does not provide.

life. One proposal is called the Europa Clipper. This satellite would orbit Jupiter, flying by Europa several times. On its way past the moon, the Europa Clipper would analyze the moon's surface, interior, and atmosphere. The satellite would also take numerous photos of Europa.

VISITING THE RED PLANET

The long-term dream of many in the space industry is to send people to visit other worlds and establish a permanent presence. Since we've already sent astronauts to the moon, the next destination is likely Mars. There is talk within NASA of

CAREER STATS

AEROSPACE ENGINEERS

MEDIAN ANNUAL SALARY (2012): $103,720

NUMBER OF JOBS (2012): 83,000

PROJECTED JOB GROWTH: 7%, slower than average

PROJECTED INCREASE IN JOBS 2012–2022: 6,100

REQUIRED EDUCATION: Bachelor's degree

LICENSE/CERTIFICATION: May be required for some positions

AEROSPACE ENGINEERING AND OPERATIONS TECHNICIANS

MEDIAN ANNUAL SALARY (2012): $61,530

NUMBER OF JOBS (2012): 9,900

PROJECTED JOB GROWTH: 0%, little or no change

PROJECTED INCREASE IN JOBS 2012–2022: 0

REQUIRED EDUCATION: Associate's degree, or certificates from vocational or technical schools

LICENSE/CERTIFICATION: May be required for some positions

PHYSICISTS AND ASTRONOMERS

MEDIAN ANNUAL SALARY (2012): $106,360

NUMBER OF JOBS (2012): 23,300

PROJECTED JOB GROWTH: 10%, as fast as average

PROJECTED INCREASE IN JOBS 2012–2022: 2,400

REQUIRED EDUCATION: Doctoral degree

LICENSE/CERTIFICATION: May be required for some positions

Figures reported by the United States Bureau of Labor Statistics

RESOURCES

BOOKS

Bailey, Diane. *The Future of Space Exploration*. Mankato, MN: Creative Education, 2013.

Carlisle, Rodney P. *Exploring Space*. New York: Chelsea House, 2010.

Flammang, James M. *Space Travel*. Ann Arbor, MI: Cherry Lake Publishing, 2009.

Paris, Stephanie. *21st Century: Mysteries of Deep Space*. Westminster, CA: Teacher Created Materials, 2013.

Sparrow, Giles. *Space Exploration*. Mankato, MN: Smart Apple Media, 2012.

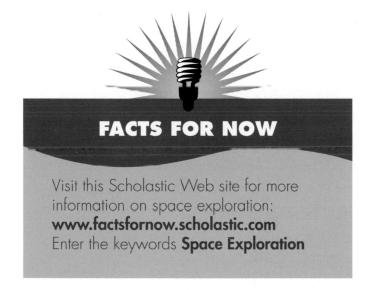

FACTS FOR NOW

Visit this Scholastic Web site for more information on space exploration:
www.factsfornow.scholastic.com
Enter the keywords **Space Exploration**

GLOSSARY

asteroids (AS-tuh-roidz) small, rocky objects that travel around the sun

astronomers (uh-STRAH-nuh-murz) scientists who study stars, planets, and space

atmosphere (AT-muhs-feer) the mixture of gases that surrounds a planet

axis (AK-sis) an imaginary line through the middle of an object, around which that object spins

core (KOR) the innermost part of a planet

dwarf planet (DWORF PLAN-it) a round heavenly body that orbits the sun or another star and is smaller than a planet

galaxy (GAL-uhk-see) a system of millions or billions of stars, together with gas and dust, held together by gravitational attraction

geysers (GYE-zurz) underground springs that shoot water and steam into the air

modular (MAHD-yoo-lur) composed of separate units that can be joined to each other in different formations

orbit (OR-bit) a curved path traveled around something, especially a planet or star

organic (or-GAN-ik) from or produced by living things

probe (PROHB) a tool or device used to explore or examine something

propulsion (pruh-PUHL-shuhn) the force by which a vehicle or some other object is moved forward

radar (RAY-dahr) a way that ships and planes find solid objects by reflecting radio waves against them and receiving the reflected waves

rover (ROH-vur) vehicle used to explore the surface of planets or moons

satellite (SAT-uh-lite) a spacecraft that is sent into orbit around a heavenly body

solar system (SOH-lur SIS-tuhm) the sun together with the eight planets, many moons, and asteroids and comets that move in orbit around it

space station (SPAYS STAY-shuhn) a spacecraft that stays in orbit and is large enough to house a crew for long periods of time

terminator (TUR-muh-nay-tur) the line between the daytime side and the nighttime side of a planet or other heavenly body orbiting a star

INDEX

Page numbers in *italics* indicate illustrations.

INDEX (CONTINUED)

ABOUT THE AUTHOR

WIL MARA'S fascination with space exploration began as a little boy sitting on the carpet of his parents' living room while watching CBS report Neil Armstrong's epic walk on the moon. Since that day, he has followed the ups and downs of NASA and other space agencies around the world with unswerving fanaticism. He is the award-winning, best-selling author of more than 150 books, many of which are educational titles for children.